THE GODS AND GODDESSES OF GREEK MYTHOLOGY

by Don Nardo

COMPASS POINT BOOKS
a capstone imprint

Compass Point Books
1710 Roe Crest Drive
North Mankato, MN 56003

Editors: Sarah Eason and Geoff Barker
Designers: Paul Myerscough and Simon Borrough
Media Researcher: Susannah Jayes
Content Consultant: Michael Vickers, DLitt., Professor of Archaeology, University of Oxford
Production Specialist: Laura Manthe

Image Credits
Alamy: The Art Gallery Collection 22, Classic Image 18–19, IML Group Ltd 34–35, Inga Leksina 20;
Bridgeman: Roy Miles Fine Art Paintings 43; **Corbis:** Bettmann 16, Araldo de Luca 46, Gianni Dagli
Orti 2–3; **Geoff Ward:** cover (front), 6, 26–27, 33, 50, 55, 59 (top left); **Getty:** The Bridgeman Art
Library 39 (front), 53; **Istockphoto:** Anthony Rosenberg chapter 3 bgd, Marisa Allegra Williams 59;
Photolibrary: Images.com 44, The Print Collector, 15; **Shutterstock:** Ananas 4–5, Ataly cover (top
bgd), chapter 1 bgd, 58, 60, Cenker Atila 58, Bryan Busovicki cover (bottom bgd), Primož Cigler 28–29
bgd, Dr Flash 8, Ben Heys 38–39, Hunor Focze 24–25, ImageZebra 48–49, Craig Jewell 14, Kamira 1,
10 (front), Andreas G Karelias 10 (back), Ralf Juergen Kraft 36 (front), Olga Matseyko 41, Nick Pavlakis
36–37, Paolo Riganti 30, Jozef Sedmak chapter 4 bgd, 64, Slimewoo 56, Irina Solatages 12–13,
Siobhan Thompson chapter 2 bgd, 62–63, Lynn Watson 29 (front).

Library of Congress Cataloging-in-Publication Data
    Nardo, Don, 1947–
    The gods and goddesses of Greek mythology / by Don Nardo.
        p. cm.—(Ancient Greek mythology)
    Includes bibliographical references and index.
    ISBN 978-0-7565-4479-9 (library binding)
    1. Mythology, Greek—Juvenile literature. 2. Gods, Greek—Juvenile
literature. 3. Goddesses, Greek—Juvenile literature. I. Title.
    BL783.N35 2012
    398.210938—dc22   2010052822

Visit Compass Point Books on the Internet at *www.capstonepub.com*

Printed in the United States of America in Stevens Point, Wisconsin.
022013   007180R

TABLE OF CONTENTS

Chapter 1
GREEK MYTH-TELLERS CELEBRATE THE GODS

Some time around the year 700 BC, a Greek farmer sat in a scenic spot on a slope of Mount Helicon and wrote a poem. A cluster of rugged peaks, Helicon is located in the region of Boeotia in south-central Greece. In those days the mountain's slopes were sacred to the Muses—nine minor goddesses who were the daughters of Zeus, leader of the Greek gods. People thought the Muses provided painters, musicians, writers, and other artists with talent and ideas.

The poetry-writing farmer was no exception. Hesiod by name, he was convinced that the Muses had inspired him to glorify the gods in verse. "The Muses once taught Hesiod to sing sweet songs," he wrote.

While [I] was shepherding [my] lambs on holy Helicon, [they] breathed a sacred voice into my mouth with which to celebrate the things to come and things which were before. They ordered me to sing [about] the race of blessed ones who live forever.

The beautiful Muses helped mortals forget their sorrows. They inspired people to create artistic works.

4

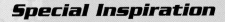

Special Inspiration

Feeling divinely motivated, Hesiod decided to pen a long poem that would honor the gods by describing their births, powers, and exploits. He called it the *Theogony*, meaning "the origins of the gods."

Hesiod Addresses the Muses

At the beginning of his long poem, the *Theogony*, Hesiod praises the Muses for their inspiration:

Hail, daughters of Zeus! Give me sweet song, to celebrate the holy race of gods who live forever, sons of starry Heaven and Earth, and gloomy Night, and salty Sea. Tell how the gods and Earth arose at first, and rivers and the boundless swollen sea and shining stars, and the broad heaven above, and how the gods divided up their wealth and how they shared their honors, how they first captured Olympus with its many folds. Tell me these things, Olympian Muses, tell from the beginning, which first came to be?

Zeus was the ruler of Mount Olympus and the Greek gods (Olympians) who lived there.

Before he started writing, Hesiod first gathered together all the stories he'd heard about these deities over the course of his life. Today we call these tales myths, from the Greek word *muthos*, meaning a spoken or written story. In addition to his other talents, therefore, Hesiod was a myth-teller. If it had not been for him and a few others like him, later ages and peoples would have known next to nothing about the Greek myths and gods.

Greek Myth-Tellers

Myth-tellers like Hesiod provided later generations with crucial knowledge about the gods the Greeks worshipped. One or more of these deities appeared in a majority of the myths. Indeed, those timeless tales both defined their personalities and described their deeds. Moreover, the most prevalent theme in Greek mythology is the colorful and often dramatic interaction between the gods and humans.

When one examines the myths about these divine beings, one is immediately struck by how much they resemble human beings. This is because the Greek gods were anthropomorphic—they possessed human form and personalities. The gods displayed human emotions, got married, had children, fought among themselves, and made most of the same mistakes that people did. Picturing the gods this way made them more understandable and approachable for the average person.

The Age of Heroes

The ancient Greeks who lived between about 800 BC and 300 BC, believed that the gods they worshipped had interacted with select humans during a period of the distant past. They called it the Age of Heroes. Today historians and other experts call it Greece's late Bronze Age, lasting from about 1500 BC to 1150 BC. They think that some of the characters of Greek mythology may have been based on real kings and other human figures from that age.

Great Powers

Yet there was one important difference between humans and the gods. The gods possessed enormous power, enough to easily destroy people and their works. A 400s BC Greek poet named Pindar stated it well:

Single is the race, single of men and of gods.
From a single mother we both draw breath. But a
difference of power in everything keeps us apart.

Demeter was the goddess of harvest, but she also brought drought to the world.

That tremendous and often magical divine power is seen frequently in the Greek myths. For example, Zeus regularly takes the forms of various animals and objects. Athena, goddess of war, uproots and tosses the island of Sicily. Demeter, overseer of plants and crops, unleashes drought and famine on humanity.

Gods Against Gods

The Greek gods used their powers not only against people but also against other gods. Also, during the famous Trojan War some gods backed the Greeks, while others helped the Trojans. By far the biggest conflict in which these divinities took part was the so-called Titanomachy. A gigantic battle that raged across the heavens and Earth, it pitted the earliest race of gods, the Titans, against a younger race, the Olympians.

The Winners

The winners of the conflict were the Olympians, led by Zeus. They are sometimes referred to as the major gods. Fourteen (or in some ancient accounts 12) in number, they were the strongest of their kind. However, numerous minor gods and goddesses existed, fulfilling a wide array of roles in nature. Among them were childbirth, sleep, health, the rainbow, the north wind, strife, the sun, youth, and death.

Homer and Hesiod

Hesiod described many of these gods, including earlier and later ones and major and minor ones. In fact, he was one of the two most important ancient Greek myth-tellers. The other was Homer. Almost nothing is known about Homer, except that he created the two greatest examples of ancient Greek literature, the *Iliad* and *Odyssey*. These monumental epics about the Trojan War and its aftermath contain thousands of references to the gods.

Homer's epic stories are nonrhyming poems written in ancient Greek.

The Gods Live On

The result was that Homer's and Hesiod's amazingly comprehensive descriptions of the gods became vital to later generations of Greeks. Herodotus, the Greek historian from the 400s BC, remarked that his two famed forerunners were

> the poets who [best] described the gods for us, giving them all their appropriate titles, offices, and powers.

Herodotus himself was among several later Greeks who wrote about the gods. His *Histories*, as its title indicates, is a work of history rather than fiction. But it frequently mentions the Greek deities, along with those of other peoples, in passing. Other important ancient writings that celebrated the gods and their exploits included the poems of Pindar (early 400s BC); the plays of the great Athenian dramatists Aeschylus, Sophocles, and Euripides (400s BC); the *Bibliotheca* of the Greek writer Apollodorus (100s BC); and the *Metamorphoses*, by the Roman poet Ovid (first centuries BC and AD). Thanks to these and other capable and diligent individuals, the Greek myths survived, thereby preserving the appearances and adventures of the gods. That has allowed these enduring tales to enchant and entertain people in each new generation. The ancient Greeks are gone, but thankfully their gods live on in books, plays, paintings, graphic novels, movies, TV shows, video games, and especially people's imaginations.

Homer and Myths

Myth-teller Homer wrote two of the greatest stories in literature. Scholars Mark Morford and Robert Lenardon described myth as "a comprehensive [term] for stories primarily concerned with the gods and man's relationship with them."

11

Chapter 2
THE RISE AND FALL OF THE TITANS

The Titans, the earliest race of gods, were not the first life-forms that existed. So they did not create the universe. According to the ancient Greek creation myths, the earliest living things were not gods in the traditional sense. That is, they were not beings with heads, bodies, arms, and legs, as were the Titans and later gods. Instead, they were vast, formless forces possessing primitive powers of perception. The first one was a huge, dark void known as Chaos. In a sense, it held the seeds of all things to come. The Roman poet Ovid, who retold the Greek myths, described it this way:

> Before land was and sea—before air and sky arched over all, all nature was all Chaos, the rounded body of all things in one. The living elements [were] at war with lifelessness. No god, no Titan shone from sky or sea ... nor was Earth poised [hanging] in air. [Rather] air [and] water heaved and turned in darkness [and] no living creatures knew that land [or] sea, where heat fell against cold, [and] heaviness fell into things that had no weight.

The Titans were the earliest race of gods, but they did not create the universe.

Dark Forces

For a long time, Chaos floated aimlessly and merely existed. Then, in ways that have never been explained, it gave rise to two more shapeless forces having a dim awareness. One was called Nyx, or Night, and the other Erebus, or Darkness. Both were black, because no light yet existed. Also, they made no sounds. So the two dark forces could not speak to each other.

The Birth of Love

Yet somehow Nyx and Erebus eventually came together. From their mysterious union sprang a more intelligent and purposeful force known as Eros, or Love. Eros swiftly sorted through the jumbled, disconnected things floating within Chaos. As a result, regions and objects having shape, form, and order began to materialize.

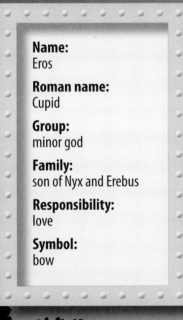

Name:
Eros

Roman name:
Cupid

Group:
minor god

Family:
son of Nyx and Erebus

Responsibility:
love

Symbol:
bow

Light, the Heavens, and Earth

Thanks to Eros, for instance, light emerged to compete with the darkness. The heavier elements, such as rocks and dirt, settled out of the void and became Earth. In contrast, the lighter elements, such as air and clouds, floated upward and formed the sky and heavens. In those heavens, the cosmic bodies appeared. These included the sun, moon, planets, and stars. On Earth, meanwhile, the land and sea became distinct from each other. Rivers flowed into seas and lakes, while trees, flowers, and other plants sprang up from the soil.

Mother Earth and Father Heaven

Deep within the fabrics of those two primary regions of existence—Earth and sky—dwelled immense spirits possessing both personality and intelligence. The spirit inhabiting Earth was named Gaea. Many ancients called her Mother Earth. Her counterpart, the spirit inhabiting the heavens, was named Uranus, sometimes called Father Heaven. It was perhaps inevitable that these two formless spirits would come to know each other.

The Titans: The First Gods

Gaea and Uranus did more than become acquainted. They mated and produced a great many children. Some of these offspring were enormous and so malformed or disfigured that they came to be seen as monsters. Each of Gaea's and Uranus' first three children, for example, had 50 heads. Also, each possessed 100 hands. So quite appropriately they came to be known as the "100-handers." Three more members of this monstrous brood were called Cyclopes, the "wheel-eyed ones." That name derived from the fact that each had a single eye in the middle of its forehead. Each Cyclops was a giant whose brawny frame would dwarf that of the average person today.

The colossal *Titanic* famously hit an iceberg in the Atlantic and sank in 1912.

Gaea and Uranus had numerous other progeny. Quite a few of them were strange, monstrous, and dangerous. But Mother Earth and Father Heaven also gave rise to some very attractive and productive children. Comprising the earliest race of gods, they became known as the Titans. Like their deformed siblings, they were large, possibly more than 30 feet (10 meters) tall. The terms titan and titanic were later applied to unusually large things, such as the famous ship the *Titanic*, or strong, accomplished people, such as the players on the Tennessee Titans football team.

Gods in Human Form

The Titans were also the first living things that had human form. In fact, when one of the Titans later created the human race, he was careful to make its members look like his own kind. The most obvious difference between the two races, of course, was that the Titans were far larger and stronger. Otherwise, these early deities were very much like people. They possessed personal flaws such as arrogance, greed, and stupidity. They also made mistakes and fought among themselves.

Beautiful Gods

Some ancient accounts say that at first there were 12 Titans and that as they had children their numbers grew. Whether or not these stories are true, the earliest gods assumed power over and responsibilities for various aspects of nature. The handsome Hyperion became god of the sun, for instance. His attractive sister, Thea, took charge of the moon and its monthly movements through the sky. (Thea's name, also spelled Theia, meant divine. It became the basis of the Greek word for the gods—*theoi*.) Later, Hyperion and Thea married and had a son, Helios. He eventually took over his father's role as the sun-god.

Rulers of the Waves

Meanwhile, the Titans Oceanus and Tethys oversaw the seas. (The word ocean later derived from Oceanus' name.) In time, these two sea gods wed, as their siblings Hyperion and Thea had, and generated numerous children. Most of the progeny of Oceanus and Tethys were minor gods and spirits associated with the seas, lakes, rivers, and other waterways.

Most Powerful

Although they were among the last Titans to spring from Gaea's womb, Cronus and Rhea ended up as the most powerful and famous. Cronus was a crude, somewhat dim-witted character. Yet he was extremely strong and ambitious, more so than any of the other Titans. So he became their leader. He took Rhea, who was smarter and kinder than he was, as his wife.

Helios is often shown with a headdress of sun rays in a chariot pulled by four horses.

17

Son against Father

One of the best-known myths about the Titans concerns Cronus' determined attempt to overthrow his father. It was no secret that Uranus hated all of his children. In particular, he disliked and wanted to get rid of the physically monstrous ones. Without warning, therefore, he snatched up the 100-handers and some of his other malformed offspring and tossed them down into Tartarus. Once inside that deepest, darkest sector of the Underworld, they were unable to escape.

When Gaea learned what her spiteful mate had done to their children, she was outraged. She loved all of her offspring, even the hideous ones. Hoping to free them from their gloomy underground prison, she called together the male Titans and, according to Hesiod, told them:

"My sons, whose father is a reckless fool, if you will do as I ask [and attack him], we shall repay [his] wicked crime." [She] spoke, but fear seized all of them, and none replied. Then crooked Cronus, growing bold, answered his well-loved mother with these words: "Mother, I [will] undertake to do the deed. I do not care for my unspeakable father, for he first thought of shameless acts." He spoke and giant [Mother] Earth was glad at heart.

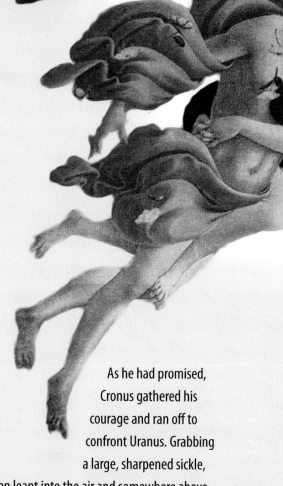

As he had promised, Cronus gathered his courage and ran off to confront Uranus. Grabbing a large, sharpened sickle, the son leapt into the air and somewhere above the clouds found and assaulted his father. The two fought for hours, as all living things watched breathlessly. Finally Cronus seriously wounded his opponent. Uranus loudly roared in pain as the swinging sickle sliced off his genitals. In a sickening display, thousands of blood droplets spurted out and showered downward. Those that touched the ground slowly but steadily grew into various living beings. Some were primitive giants and others were frightening flying creatures with sharp teeth and claws.

Italian artist Botticelli painted the birth of Venus (the Roman name for Aphrodite).

Meanwhile, the mutilated genitals landed in the sea. There, they gave rise to something unexpected and astoundingly beautiful. In Hesiod's words:

> Thrown [into] the stormy sea, [the organs] were carried for a long time on the waves. White foam surrounded the immortal flesh, and in it grew a girl. [Near the island of Cyprus] the goddess came forth, lovely, much revered, and grass grew up beneath her delicate feet. Her name [was] Aphrodite.

As this lovely deity (who would later be called the goddess of love) walked out onto dry land, Cronus finished the fight with Uranus. The latter finally lay injured and defeated. Wasting no time, his

Name:
Aphrodite

Roman name:
Venus

Group:
Olympian

Family:
sister of Zeus

Responsibility:
love and beauty

Symbols:
swan, dove

The name of the great Greek Titan Cronus is also spelled Cronos.

The Turbulent Titanomachy

With Uranus removed from the scene, Cronus took charge of the universe. Not long afterward, Cronus' divine mate, Rhea, announced that she was about to produce several offspring. However, the leader of the gods suddenly had second thoughts about the idea of fatherhood. Thinking back to what he had done to his father, he worried that his own children might attack and defeat him in the same manner. Hoping to prevent such a rebellion from happening, Cronus resorted to a bizarre extreme. When the first child was born, he thrust it into his immense mouth and swallowed it. Because the infant was a god, it was immortal, so it didn't die.

Name:
Cronus

Roman name:
Saturn

Group:
Titan

Family:
son of Uranus and Gaea, husband of Rhea, father of Zeus

Responsibility:
time and the ages

Symbol:
sickle

Instead, it remained inside Cronus' big body, where over time it continued to grow. Rhea was extremely distressed when her husband swallowed the next four children in the same manner. Realizing that a sixth one was on the way, in despair she decided to save it from the others' fate. She gave birth to the child, a boy, in secret and hid it in a cave on the large Greek island of Crete. Also, at the moment when Cronus was expecting the child to be delivered, she fooled him. Draping baby's clothes around a large stone, she handed it to him and he shoved it down his throat without even looking at it. Cronus then went about his business. He had no idea that the real child was quietly being raised by some of Gaea's female offspring in faraway Crete. The boy, whose name was Zeus, was destined to radically change the course of divine history.

Zeus to the Rescue

When Zeus reached young manhood, he set out to save his swallowed siblings. With the aid of his grandmother, Gaea, he secretly slipped his father a drug that made him get sick to his stomach. Cronus suddenly vomited and out popped the big stone he had gulped down years before. Then came his first five children, who were now fully grown— Demeter, Hestia, Hera, Poseidon, and Hades. Along with Zeus, they formed the nucleus of a new race of gods. Their number soon became seven when Zeus' daughter, Athena, clad in a suit of armor, suddenly sprang from his head.

Determined to overthrow Cronus and the Titans who supported him, the younger gods attacked them. Zeus and his brothers and sisters were not alone in the fight. For various reasons, Oceanus, Tethys, Prometheus, and a few other Titans intensely disliked Cronus. So they switched sides and fought against their own kind. In addition, Prometheus told Zeus how to release the 100-handers and other monsters that both Uranus and Cronus had kept locked up in Tartarus. These creatures also aided Zeus.

Name:
Prometheus

Roman name:
Prometheus

Group:
Titan

Family:
son of Titans Iapetus
and Themis

Responsibility:
created first humans
from clay

Symbol:
torch

Bitter Battles

Yet even with the extra help, Zeus and his followers found Cronus and his own forces incredibly hard to defeat. The terribly turbulent war, which would later come to be called the Titanomachy, raged on year after year. Hesiod later wrote about it, as did several other ancient writers. One particularly expressive version was penned by a Greek from the 300s AD named Quintus Smyrnaeus. He said in part:

The immortals [younger gods] all around fierce-battling with the Titans fought for Zeus. Already were their foes enwrapped with flame, for thick and fast as snowflakes poured from heaven [Zeus'] thunderbolts. The might of Zeus was roused [against] the presumptuous Titans. [He] poured down fire from heaven, then burned all earth beneath, and Oceanus' world-engirdling flood boiled from its depths, yea, to its utmost bounds. Far-flowing mighty rivers were dried up . . . Smoke and ashes veiled the air; earth fainted in the fervent heat.

The Creatures of Prometheus

Prometheus, who was the son of the Titans Iapetus and Themis, became an ally of Zeus during the war between the Titans and Olympians. After it was over, Prometheus created the bodies of the first humans out of clay. The goddess Athena helped him bring them to life. On learning about these so-called creatures of Prometheus, Zeus ordered that they should never be given knowledge of fire, since that gift was reserved for the gods. However, Prometheus pitied his creations, whose lives were very difficult without the use of fire. He secretly stole some fire from the heavens and gave it to them. Zeus soon found out and punished Prometheus by having him chained to the top of a mountain. There, a huge vulture landed each day and ate the Titan's liver, which grew back each night. Prometheus' agonies on the mountain are the subject of the powerful play Prometheus Bound.

"The Whole Earth Broiled"

Several ancient writers wrote colorful descriptions of the Titanomachy, the War of the Titans. Part of Hesiod's version, in his Theogony, *states:* "The boundless sea roared terribly around, the great Earth rumbled, and broad heaven groaned, shaken. And tall Olympus was disturbed down to its roots, when the immortals charged. The heavy quaking from their footsteps reached down to dark Tartarus, and piercing sounds of awful battle, and their mighty shafts. They hurled their wounding missiles, and the voices of both sides, shouting, reached the starry sky … The fertile Earth, being burnt, roared out, [and] the voiceless forest cried and crackled with fire. The whole Earth broiled."

The Winners

Finally, after 10 years of enormously violent strife, Zeus' forces achieved victory. Wasting no time, they hurled Cronus and his backers into the dismal depths of Tartarus. There, at Zeus' order, the fearsome 100-handers stood guard to ensure that the defeated Titans could never escape. Then the winners of the war proceeded to take charge of the universe. They, along with some of their children, became known as the Olympian gods. They were fated to deal with a new race of beings called humans, who would variously worship, envy, and curse them for untold ages to come.

Chapter 3

MIGHTY ZEUS AND THE OLYMPIAN GODS

Following their great victory over the Titans, Zeus and his companions took charge of the known universe, including Earth. They erected splendid palaces for themselves atop Greece's highest peak—Mount Olympus. For that reason, they became known as the Olympians.

Retaining the leadership role he had played during the revolt against the Titans, Zeus became the leader of the Olympian gods. He made his sister, Hera, his wife. So thereafter she was widely referred to as the queen of the gods. Zeus' two brothers, Poseidon and Hades, had demanded and received considerable authority of their own. Poseidon became ruler of the seas, while Hades took charge of the Underworld.

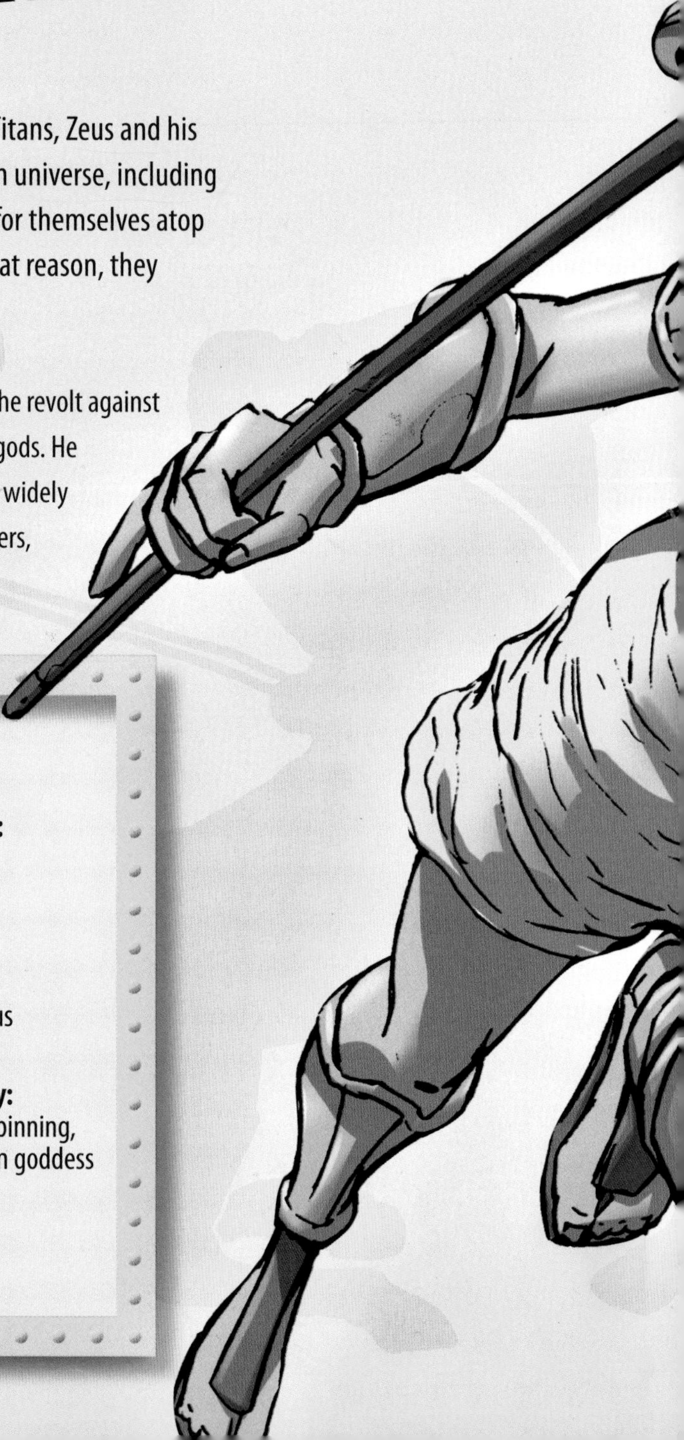

Name:
Athena

Roman name:
Minerva

Group:
Olympian

Family:
daughter of Zeus and Metis

Responsibility:
war, wisdom; spinning, weaving; patron goddess of Athens

Symbols:
owl, olive tree

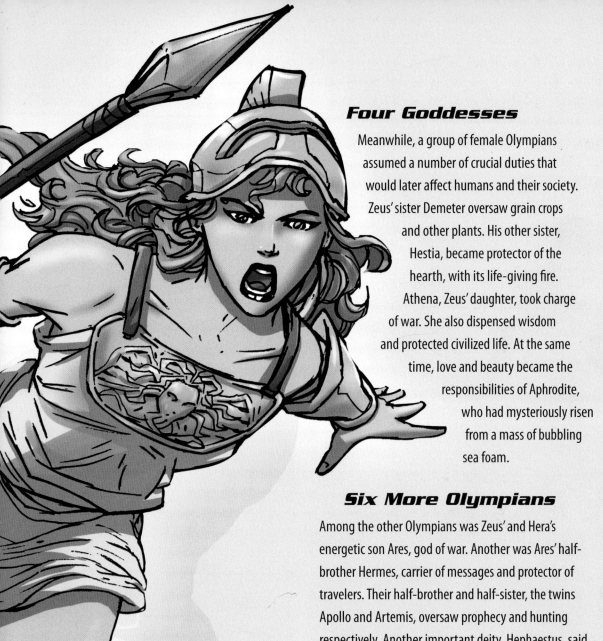

Four Goddesses

Meanwhile, a group of female Olympians assumed a number of crucial duties that would later affect humans and their society. Zeus' sister Demeter oversaw grain crops and other plants. His other sister, Hestia, became protector of the hearth, with its life-giving fire. Athena, Zeus' daughter, took charge of war. She also dispensed wisdom and protected civilized life. At the same time, love and beauty became the responsibilities of Aphrodite, who had mysteriously risen from a mass of bubbling sea foam.

Six More Olympians

Among the other Olympians was Zeus' and Hera's energetic son Ares, god of war. Another was Ares' half-brother Hermes, carrier of messages and protector of travelers. Their half-brother and half-sister, the twins Apollo and Artemis, oversaw prophecy and hunting respectively. Another important deity, Hephaestus, said to have been begotten by Hera alone, was the god of forges and protector of craftsmen. The last Olympian, Zeus' son Dionysus, was god of vines and the fertility of the soil. (Some ancient writers claimed that the Olympians numbered 12 rather than 14. This may have been because Hestia and Demeter eventually left Olympus and made their homes on Earth.)

Usually shown in armor, the great goddess Athena was involved in the Trojan War.

King and Queen of the Gods

Of the many myths in which the Olympian gods took part, a hefty proportion involved Zeus, the leader of those deities, and Hera, his sister and later wife. The ancient Greeks held that Zeus (whom the Romans called Jupiter) controlled several natural forces, including thunder, lightning, and rain. Appropriately, one of his symbols was the thunderbolt, which he was said to wield as a weapon. The Greeks also credited Zeus with being in charge of laws, justice, and morality. Accordingly, another of his symbols was the oak tree, based on a sacred oak that grew at his temple at Dodona, in northwestern Greece. The priestesses at Dodona were said to pass on messages from Zeus relating to justice, morality, and related topics.

One of the Seven Wonders

Other shrines to Zeus existed all across Greece. Perhaps the most renowned was the Temple of Olympian Zeus at Olympia, in southwestern Greece. It was there that the ancient Olympic Games took place every four years. Inside the temple was an enormous statue of the god, crafted by the Athenian sculptor Phidias in the 400s BC. Later it was named one of the Seven Wonders of the Ancient World. Like other ancient artists, Phidias portrayed Zeus as bearded, with an imposing, muscular frame.

Female Protector

In addition to her role as queen of Mount Olympus, Hera (whom the Romans called Juno), was seen as the protector of marriage and women's life. Among her symbols was the pomegranate. This derived from a custom practiced in Athens and some other Greek city-states. To celebrate a wedding, people gave pomegranates to the bride in Hera's name. In addition, a majority of weddings were held in Gamelion (January), the Greek month honoring Hera. Greek artists most often pictured her as a mature yet still beautiful woman

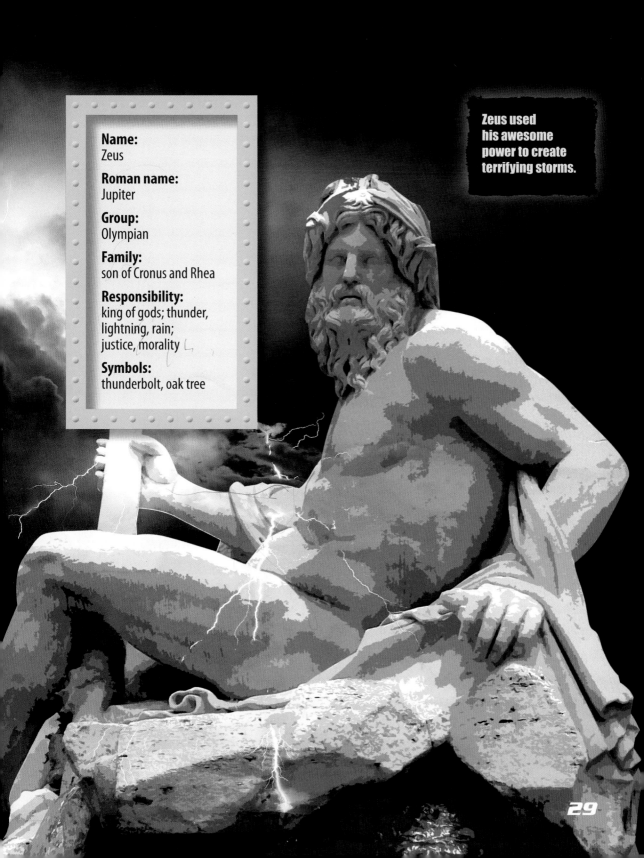

Name:
Zeus

Roman name:
Jupiter

Group:
Olympian

Family:
son of Cronus and Rhea

Responsibility:
king of gods; thunder,
lightning, rain;
justice, morality

Symbols:
thunderbolt, oak tree

Zeus used
his awesome
power to create
terrifying storms.

One of Zeus' most famous disguises was as a swan. He transformed himself into the beautiful bird to seduce the Spartan queen Leda.

Zeus and His Lovers

Both Zeus and Hera appeared separately in a number of myths. Also, some myths featured both of them. Nearly all of these dealt with his frequent love affairs with other women, usually mortals, and her jealousy and efforts to punish those women. When approaching other women, Zeus often took the form of a mortal man. He was also known to assume the forms of creatures and objects, including a swan, a bull, and a cloud of gold dust. In the case of Semele, daughter of Cadmus, founder of Thebes, Zeus pretended to be a handsome young man. The attractive young Semele fell in love with the stranger and became pregnant by him.

Hera's Punishment

As she always did, Hera found out what her husband had done and immediately devised a plan to punish Semele. The goddess fooled the young women by using one of Zeus' own tricks—taking human form. According to the ancient myth-teller Ovid, Hera *"took care [to] simulate old age, take on gray hair, a wrinkled skin, bent back, and feebleness as she . . . assumed the voice of Semele's old nurse, Beroe."* The disguised goddess urged the girl to ask her lover to appear to her in his true form. *"'Make him prove his love,'* Hera said. *'Make him appear before you in the same fashion as when queen Hera takes him in her arms. Tell him to take you as he is in heaven, dressed in his glory!'"*

Name:
Hera

Roman name:
Juno

Group:
Olympian

Family:
daughter of Cronus and Gaea, sister and wife of Zeus

Responsibility:
queen of gods; women and marriage

Symbol:
pomegranate

Unfortunately for Semele, she followed this advice. The next time she saw Zeus, she begged him to show himself as he really was and reluctantly he did so. But his true form was so bright and intense that the young woman felt herself burning up. Seeing her turning into ashes, the god suddenly thought about the baby—his own child—in her womb. As swiftly as he could, he grabbed hold of the infant and pulled it free, saving it in the nick of time.

Zeus Saves His Child

Zeus was worried that Hera might try to harm the baby. So he sliced open his own thigh, stuffed the child inside the wound, and sewed it up. A few weeks later, the god Dionysus (whom the Romans called Bacchus) emerged from Zeus' thigh. For the time being, to keep the divine youngster safe, the leader of the gods hid him in a cave. (Later, when grown, Dionysus rescued his mother, Semele, from the Underworld. He brought her to Mount Olympus, where Zeus granted her immortality.)

Apollo and Artemis

Dionysus was only one of several divine or semidivine children Zeus sired. Among the more famous of those exceptional beings were Apollo and Artemis (Diana to the Romans).

Apollo and Artemis were twins born of the female Titan Leto, who had mated with Zeus. According to most ancient writers, the double birth took place on Delos, a small island near the center of the Aegean Sea. The two divine children were given magical substances to eat, so they grew into adults in just a few days.

Name:
Apollo

Roman name:
Apollo

Group:
Olympian

Family:
son of Zeus and Leto, brother of Artemis

Responsibility:
poetry, healing, music, archery

Symbol:
laurel tree

Apollo was the most versatile of the gods. He oversaw prophecy, poetry, healing, music, and archery. His main symbol was the laurel tree, and Greek artists often depicted him with laurel leaves in his hair. Artemis was fairly versatile in her own right. She was the goddess of wild animals, hunting, and archery, and she protected young girls. Her symbols were the cypress tree, the deer, and the dog. Fittingly, artists frequently showed dogs or other animals accompanying her as she wielded her hunting bow.

Apollo was exceptional in many fields, including archery.

Niobe's Insult

Like most children, both mortal and divine, Apollo and Artemis were very protective of their mother. So they were extremely upset when they received some distressing news. Niobe, who was the wife of Amphion—one of the builders of Thebes—had badly insulted Leto. Niobe had seven sons and seven daughters, all attractive and healthy. But though blessed by so many fine children, she also had a serious character flaw, namely enormous arrogance. One day Niobe went to Leto's temple in Thebes and addressed some women who were praying. These worshippers should abandon Leto, she said. They should start worshipping Niobe instead. After all, she had 14 children, whereas Leto had only two.

Revenge of the Twins

News of this offense against Leto quickly reached her and she hurried to her twins and told them what had happened. Both Apollo and Artemis were outraged, and became determined to punish the insolent Niobe. From Olympus' steep heights, they swooped downward and reached distant Thebes in mere minutes. Less than

Name:
Artemis

Roman name:
Diana

Group:
Olympian

Family:
daughter of Zeus and Leto; sister of Apollo

Responsibility:
hunting, archery, young girls

Symbols:
bow, cypress tree, deer, dog

Mount Olympus was home to many Greek deities. Apollo and Artemis both lived there.

another minute elapsed before they had located Niobe and her 14 offspring. Readying their deadly bows, the two gods let loose an incredible flurry of arrows, which rained down on the woman's seven sons, killing all of them. Having accomplished this gory deed, Apollo and Artemis felt that they had achieved their vengeance for their mother. But as they turned to go, Niobe made things worse by loudly cursing and defying them. This made the deities angry once more, and they turned on Niobe's daughters. As Ovid described it:

> The twang of the bowstrings rang out, bringing terror. The sisters, with their hair flowing and dressed in black, were standing where their brothers lay in death. One, as she pulled the arrow from his flesh, fell dying as she tried to kiss her brother's lips. A second, endeavoring to console her mother in her misery, suddenly fell silent and doubled up with a hidden wound. One sank down as she tried in vain to escape; another fell dead upon her sister. One tried to hide; another stood there trembling. When six had been taken by death suffering various sorts of wounds, only one remained. Then the mother, shielding this last child with her body and covering her with her cloak, cried out, "Leave this one for me, leave me the youngest one! I pray you, leave the smallest, leave one!"
> But even as she prayed, the one she prayed to save fell dead.

Niobe learned the hard way that humans would pay a heavy price for disrespecting the immortal gods.

Patron and Protector of Athens

One of those powerful deities was respected far more often than she was *dis*respected. She was Athena (the Romans called her Minerva.) The goddess of war and wisdom, she also oversaw spinning, weaving, and a number of other crafts associated with human cities and civilization. In addition, she was the patron goddess of Greece's most famous and populous city, Athens.

The Owl

Both of Athena's chief symbols—the owl and the olive tree—played central roles in Athenian life. To honor the goddess, the people of Athens adopted the owl as a trademark, particularly by putting the image of that bird on their coins. A 400s BC Athenian silver coin became widely known as an "owl."

Famous Temples

Athena's other major symbol, the olive tree, derived from a well-known Athenian myth. The myth claimed that many centuries before, during the legendary Age of Heroes, Athena had hurled a wooden statue of herself out of the sky. Supposedly it had landed on Athens' central, rocky hill, the Acropolis. The particular spot it struck later became the site for a succession of temples in which the Athenians kept and worshipped the sacred statue. Each temple on the spot was named the Erechtheum. The other famous temple honoring Athena on the Acropolis was the magnificent Parthenon. Inside its main room, called a cella, stood a 40 foot- (12 meter-) tall statue of the goddess. Created by the sculptor Phidias, it was constructed of wood covered with sheets of beaten gold and ivory.

From the Head of Zeus

Another early myth about Athena described her miraculous birth. The 700s BC myth-teller Hesiod described it this way:

Zeus, the king of the gods, first made the Titan Metis his wife, and in truth she was very wise. But Zeus deceived Metis [and] swallowed her, [for] it was decreed by fate that very thoughtful children would be born of Metis, and the first to be born would be the bright-eyed maiden Athena, who would have strength and wisdom equal to her father's. [Metis] remained concealed within the innermost parts of Zeus [and against his own will he eventually] brought [Athena] into the world . . . clad in the armor of war, from out of his head.

Dedicated to the Greek goddess Athena, the great Parthenon housed her magnificent sculpture.

Athena against Poseidon

Still another well-known myth about Athena dealt with a contest she had with the lord of the seas, Poseidon (the Roman Neptune). It was said to have taken place long ago, when the Athenians did not yet have a divine patron. A city's patron god or goddess had a special fondness for that place and its people. He or she watched over the city. Also, from time to time the patron deity spent time in one or more of the temples built for him or her by the local citizenry. (To respect the god's or goddess' privacy, therefore, worship took place outside, rather than inside, the temple.)

Contest on the Acropolis

Athena badly wanted to become the patron of Athens. But so did Poseidon. So the two agreed to stage a competition. Each would produce something wondrous atop the Athenian Acropolis, while Zeus and several other Olympians acted as judges. Whichever of the two competing deities the judges chose would become the city's patron.

When the appointed day arrived, all the Athenians crowded around the Acropolis to watch the contest. As Zeus and the other judges looked on from high above, Athena and Poseidon arrived. Their enormous bodies dwarfed those of the awed spectators. In a single bound the two contestants ascended the hill and glared defiantly at each other.

Poseidon's enduring symbol is his trident, the three-pronged spear he bears.

Poseidon Steps Up

Seconds later, at a signal from Zeus, the contest began. Poseidon grasped his trident, the three-pronged spear that was one of his chief symbols. Dramatically, he held the weapon high, then slowly walked across the hilltop until he found just the right spot. As soon as he touched his trident to that spot, a saltwater spring miraculously gushed from it. The human spectators applauded loudly. Meanwhile, up above the Olympian judges nodded their approval.

Athena's Turn

Then it was Athena's turn. Wearing her signature shining breastplate, she too strode across the hilltop. Seemingly she was searching for a special spot, and eventually she found it. Then she reached out her hand and pointed a finger at the ground. At first, nothing happened. But soon a tiny twig popped upward from the dirt. As the fascinated onlookers watched, it twisted, turned, and grew larger, sprouting branches and leaves until it became a small tree. It was no ordinary tree, however, but the world's first olive tree. Cuttings from it could be planted to produce thousands more like it. As a result, the Athenians and other Greeks would enjoy the numerous practical uses of olive oil, from fuel for lamps to a basic ingredient of soaps and perfumes.

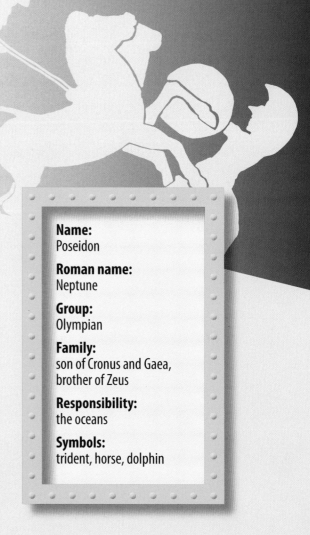

Name:
Poseidon

Roman name:
Neptune

Group:
Olympian

Family:
son of Cronus and Gaea, brother of Zeus

Responsibility:
the oceans

Symbols:
trident, horse, dolphin

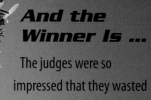

And the Winner Is ...

The judges were so impressed that they wasted no time in declaring Athena the winner. She became the patron of Athens and thereafter was often called Athena Polias, meaning Athena of the City. Throughout the remainder of the Age of Heroes, she continued to interact directly with humans. Most of the other Olympians did the same. It was that contact between mortals and gods that filled the Greeks in later ages with wonder when they recalled that marvelous bygone era.

The olive tree is one of the few trees that can produce fruit on rocky land.

Chapter 4
A VAST NUMBER OF MINOR GODS

The Titans and Olympians were undoubtedly the most important gods in ancient Greek religion and mythology. However, they were not the only superhuman beings that existed in the Greek pantheon, the group of gods. The Greeks held that a vast number of minor deities also inhabited Earth and the universe. Some, like the nymphs and Muses, were members of groups. It was the Muses, those suppliers of artistic talents, who had inspired the Greek poet Hesiod. Other minor divinities, including Eros, god of love, and Nike, goddess of victory, existed singly.

Love and Victory

Also, some minor gods played important roles in well-known myths. Eros was a good example. He was a leading character in one of the most famous and charming of all the ancient myths. By contrast, Nike had no major myths. In fact, other than a very small role in Hesiod's version of the Titanomachy, she did not appear in any stories handed down from the Age of Heroes. Yet she was highly revered by the classical Greeks, who frequently depicted her in their art. Her powerful reputation in later ages showed that even a minor deity with no myths could, over time, achieve widespread popularity.

The Nymphs

Among the minor deities who did
appear often in popular myths, the
nymphs, all of whom were female,
were the most numerous. Indeed,
they numbered in the thousands.
These goddesses were seen to dwell
within, or represent, specific niches
or aspects of nature. Among others,
these included trees, meadows,
caves, wells, lakes, clouds,
and beaches.

Nymphs were
not immortal
goddesses, but
they were still
able to live for
a very long time.

Nymphs

Nymphs were beautiful nature spirits of Greek mythology. They were often seen in the company of major gods, such as Dionysus, the god of vines and fertility, and Artemis, the goddess of hunting, archery, and young girls.

Daughters of Zeus

According to ancient writers, most of the nymphs were daughters of Zeus. He was said to have mated with various female Titans to produce them. However, a few nymphs were offspring of other deities. For example, three groups of these goddesses—the Hesperides, Hyades, and Pleiades—were children of the Titan Atlas. Also, the Titans Oceanus and Tethys, who sided with Zeus in the Titanomachy, were the parents of a group of sea nymphs called the Oceanids. Among the numerous other groups of nymphs were the Dryades, who inhabited trees; the Oreades (mountains); Naiades (lakes); Epimelides (highland pastures); Potameides (rivers); and Haliai (sands and rocky shores).

Beautiful Appearance

As for their appearance, virtually all nymphs were beautiful young women with well-proportioned bodies. This was certainly the way that ancient Greek painters and sculptors portrayed them. About their characters, the noted classical scholar Michael Grant writes:

> They possessed an amorous [romantic] disposition, and were credited with many love affairs with gods and men, resulting in the births of numerous children. [Most nymphs were] found in the company of gods, especially Pan, Hermes, Apollo, Dionysus, and Artemis, and in association with satyrs [creatures half man and half goat]. They resemble the fairies of later folklore and, like them, could be cruel as well as kind.

Of the cruel nymphs Grant mentions, one was a river goddess named Nais. When she learned that her lover, a herdsman called Daphnis, had had an affair with a mortal woman, she blinded him. Spiteful nymphs of this sort were rare, however. Most were kind-hearted and good-natured.

Narcissus is famous for falling in love with his own reflection in a pool of water.

Echo and Narcissus

Although nymphs of one sort or another appeared in many myths, they were rarely central characters in those stories. One exception was the nymph named Echo. She made her home on the slopes of Mount Helicon, not far from where Hesiod lived. Echo was not only physically attractive, but also very kind. She did have one character flaw, however: She was extremely talkative, so much so that nearly everyone she met grew irritated with her.

One of those who became annoyed with Echo was the queen of the gods, Hera. One day Hera was trying to spy on her husband, Zeus, whom she suspected of being unfaithful to her. But Echo, who had accompanied the goddess, was her usual chatty self. The result was that Zeus heard Echo's voice and realized that Hera was watching him. Hera was so angry with Echo for this that she decided to punish her. From then on, Hera said, Echo would only be able to repeat the last syllables of whatever words people spoke to her.

It turned out that this was only the beginning of Echo's troubles. A few months later, she fell in love with a good-looking but highly self-centered young man named Narcissus. He rejected her, causing her to fall into a state of extreme depression in which she refused to eat. Slowly but steadily she wasted away. Finally, all that was left was her voice, which continued repeating the last things people said. This was supposedly the source of the natural phenomenon named for her—the echo.

Orpheus and Eurydice

Another famous myth in which a nymph played a leading role was the tale of Orpheus and Eurydice. Eurydice was one of the Dryades, nymphs who tended to the health of trees. One day she met a young man named Orpheus. As the son of the Muse Calliope, he was semidivine. Also, because his mother inspired musical ability in selected humans, he became a fantastically talented musician. It was said that when he played his harp all people—and even animals, rocks, and trees—became spellbound, unable to stop listening.

Eurydice and Orpheus fell in love practically at first sight, and not long afterward they married. But their happiness did not last long. She was bitten by a poisonous snake and died, soon after which Thanatus, god of death, led her into the Underworld.

Name:
Eurydice

Roman name:
Eurydice

Group:
Dryades (nymphs)

Family:
daughter of Apollo

Responsibility:
oak tree nymph

Symbol:
snake

47

Descent into the Underworld

Orpheus was so distressed over his loss that he refused to accept Eurydice's death. In a bold move, he descended into the dark realm of the dead. There, he played his harp for the ruler of the Underworld, Hades. The music was so enchanting and sad that Hades was moved to tears. He agreed to allow Eurydice to return to the land of the living on one condition. She must walk behind her husband. Moreover, he must never look back at her until they had reached the sunlit surface. Orpheus obeyed Hades' command during most of the long upward trek. But at the last moment, the man gave in to temptation and looked back. The instant he did so, Eurydice was yanked backward into the underground caverns, and he never saw her again.

Beautiful Vision

Unlike the nymphs and Muses, the god of love, Eros, was not part of a group of deities. In fact, he mostly kept to himself and usually answered to no one. There were several ancient traditions about Eros. The best-known held that he was the son of Aphrodite, goddess of love, and Ares, god of war.

With Aphrodite as a mother, it is not surprising that Eros was extremely good-looking. He was also a gifted athlete and expert with a bow, which became his chief symbol.

Name:
Orpheus

Roman name:
Orpheus

Group:
Greek mortal

Family:
son of Apollo and the
Muse Calliope

Responsibility:
making music

Symbol:
lyre (harp)

In the most famous myth about Eros, he and his mother are referred to by their Roman names, Cupid and Venus. The Roman writer Apuleius told the romantic story, "Cupid and Psyche," in his novel, *The Golden Ass*. It begins in a faraway kingdom, whose ruler had three beautiful daughters. The youngest of the three, Psyche, was so gorgeous that the kingdom's inhabitants started offering prayers to her instead of to the love-goddess Venus.

The Roman god Cupid is often shown in cherubic form.

Furious Venus sent her son Cupid to punish Psyche, but her plan failed.

The Jealous Goddess of Love

When Venus found out what was happening, she was fuming with anger. She summoned her handsome son Cupid and ordered him to punish Psyche. He was to make her fall in love with the ugliest, meanest, most brutal man in the world, which would cause her to have a miserable life.

Cupid started out intending to do as his divine mother had ordered. But when he first saw Psyche, he instantly fell in love with her. He arranged for her to make her way to a small palace in the center of a deserted valley. When Psyche entered the splendidly furnished building, she heard a male voice. He told her to make herself at home, to enjoy a lavish meal that had been prepared for her, and to retire to bed. She did as the voice instructed.

Night Visitor

Later that evening, when she was in bed, Psyche felt someone lie beside her. Because it was dark, she could not tell who it was. But she did recognize his voice as the one she had heard earlier. They talked for hours and became friends. This went on night after night, until Psyche fell in love with her visitor, although she still had never seen what he looked like. He then asked her to marry him. His condition was that he must continue to remain unseen. Somewhat reluctantly, she agreed, and they were happy for several months.

Fear of a Hideous Monster

In the meantime, Psyche's two sisters had been looking for her. They eventually found her in the palace and asked her what she'd been doing. When she told them about her new husband who always remained in the shadows, they were appalled. They said that he would not be hiding himself that way unless something was wrong with him. He might be a hideous monster, they said. She should wait until he was asleep, shine a lamp on him, and stab him to death.

Fearing her sisters might be right, that night Psyche waited until her husband had fallen asleep. She found a lamp and a knife and nervously went to him. But as Apuleius told it, when she shone the lamp on him,

> she beheld of all beasts the gentlest and sweetest, Cupid himself, a handsome god lying in a handsome posture. Even the lamplight was cheered and brightened on sighting him. [As] for Psyche, she was awe-struck at this wonderful vision.

Betrayal

Cupid soon awakened. He angrily told Psyche that she had betrayed his trust and left her sobbing in the palace. Venus soon found out that her son had married Psyche instead of punishing her. The goddess was furious. So when Psyche visited her and begged for her forgiveness, Venus was not yet ready to pardon the young woman. The deity assigned Psyche a number of extremely difficult tasks, saying that only if she completed them would the pardon be granted. Venus assumed that the girl would never be able to finish the tasks. However, the diligent Psyche did so. This only made the goddess even more angry, and she further punished Psyche by putting her into a deep sleep.

Cupid fell for lovely Psyche, despite the best efforts of his mother Venus to stop him.

Cupid to the Rescue

At this point, Cupid heard what his mother had been doing to Psyche. He revived his wife from the spell. Then he went to Jupiter (the Roman name for Zeus) and asked him for help in dealing with Venus.

Jupiter offered to make Psyche immortal, like the gods, and Venus' anger soon dissipated. Thereafter, Cupid and the wife he adored enjoyed eternal happiness.

Thanatus

Another of the minor gods was destined never to know the kind of happy endings that Cupid enjoyed. Thanatus, the dismal deity who led the deceased down into the Underworld, was always dealing with sorrowful souls. After all, almost no one was happy about dying. In fact, from time to time human souls tried to resist or outwit Thanatus, whom Greek artists pictured as a muscular man wearing a black robe.

Defying Death

The most famous myth about Thanatus dealt with a case in which someone did successfully resist him. Admetus, king of Pherae, in central Greece, was close to death. At the last moment, his beautiful and loving wife, Alcestis, selflessly volunteered to die in his place. Alerted to what was happening, Thanatus made his way to Pherae to claim Alcestis' soul.

Greek Name:
Thanatos

Roman name:
Thanatus

Group:
minor god

Family:
son of Nyx and Erebus

Responsibility:
entry to Underworld

Symbol:
upside-down torch

Minor Greek god Thanatus personified death. Few were able to defeat or outwit him.

The Mighty Heracles

To everyone's surprise, however, at the same time an unexpected visitor arrived at Admetus' palace. The stranger was none other than the semidivine strongman Heracles (the Roman Hercules). Hearing about Alcestis' heroic gesture, Heracles became determined to deprive Thanatus of her soul. When the god of death arrived, the strongman pounced on him and the two wrestled feverishly for hours.

Finally, the bruised and panting Thanatus could take no more. He conceded the fight to the mighty Heracles and returned to the Underworld. Alcestis was reunited with her husband and they enjoyed several more years of happy life together. The story of Thanatus, Alcestis, and Heracles showed that in the Age of Heroes, when gods regularly interacted with humans, fate and death did not always have the final word. From time to time, they could be cheated or conquered by the powers of love, unselfishness, and fearless courage.

A world-famous, headless statue of Nike is displayed in the Louvre Museum in Paris.

Nike: Bringer of Victory

Nike, the Greek goddess of victory, was especially popular during the 400s BC, when Greece was invaded by huge armies from Persia (in today's Iran, Iraq, Syria, and Turkey). Nike became a major subject of sculptors and painters, who usually pictured her with wings. The most famous of these artistic works was a human-sized figure of her carved by the great Athenian sculptor Phidias. The figure stood upright in the open palm of his giant statue of Athena inside the Parthenon. Athenians and other Greeks also often prayed to Nike, usually asking her to bring them victory in battle. A surviving hymn, composed to her sometime between the 200s BC and the 100s AD, goes:

O powerful Nike, by men desired, [you] I invoke, whose might alone can quell contending rage. [It is your task] in battle to confer the crown, the victor's prize, the mark of sweet renown, for thou rulest all things, Nike divine! And glorious strife, and joyful shouts are thine. Come, mighty goddess, and thy suppliant [worshipper] bless, with sparkling eyes, elated with success. May deeds illustrious thy protection claim, and find, led on by thee, immortal fame.

TITANS, OLYMPIANS, AND OTHER GODS

Titans

Atlas
Coeus
Crius
Cronus
Epimetheus
Hyperion
Lapetus
Menoetius
Mnemosyne
Oceanus
Phoebe
Prometheus
Rhea
Tethys
Thea
Themis

Olympians

Aphrodite
Apollo
Ares
Artemis
Athena
Demeter
Dionysus
Hades
Hephaestus
Hera
Hermes
Hestia
Poseidon
Zeus

Minor Deities

Eros

Heracles

Nike

Orpheus

Thanatus

Nymphs

Echo

Eurydice

Nais

Muses

Calliope

Clio

Erato

Euterpe

Melpomene

Polyhymnia

Terpsichore

Thalia

Urania

ADDITIONAL RESOURCES

Further Reading

Daly, Kathleen N. *Greek and Roman Mythology A to Z*. New York: Chelsea House, 2009.

Hamby, Zachary. *Mythology for Teens: Classic Myths for Today's World*. Austin, Texas: Prufrock Press, 2009.

O'Connor, George. *Zeus: King of the Gods*. New York: First Second, 2010.

Orr, Tamara. *Apollo*. Hockessin, Del.: Mitchell Lane, 2008.

Roberts, Russell. *Poseidon*. Hockessin, Del.: Mitchell Lane, 2008.

Warner, Rex. *Men and Gods*. New York: NYRB, 2008.

Internet Sites

Use FactHound to find Internet sites related to this book. All of the sites on FactHound have been researched by our staff.

Here's all you do:
Visit *www.facthound.com*
Type in this code:
9780756544799

GLOSSARY

Age of Heroes the period of the dim past in which the classical Greeks believed the stories told in their myths took place. Modern scholars call that era Greece's late Bronze Age and date it from about 1500 BC to 1150 BC

ally a friend in battle

anthropomorphism attributing human personalities or traits to animals or nonliving things

cella the main room of an ancient Greek temple

classical Greeks modern scholars date Greece's Classical Age to about 500 BC to 323 BC. More generally, the inhabitants of Greece between about 800 BC and 300 BC.

epic a long poem, usually describing heroic acts

genitals the private parts, exterior sexual organs

honor to respect, or worship

immortality a state of living forever

morality the quality of being moral, knowing right from wrong

mortal a human being

Muses nine sister goddesses who protected various arts and inspired humans

mythology a group of stories about gods, monsters, heroes, and strangely shaped or fantastic creatures

nymph one of several groups of minor nature goddesses

Olympians the group of gods led by Zeus and thought to live on top of Mount Olympus, Greece's highest mountain

pantheon a group of gods worshipped by a people or nation

patron god or goddess in the ancient world, a deity who watched over and protected a specific city and its inhabitants

primitive crude, early

progeny children or offspring

prophecy the art or process of foretelling the future; or a specific prediction

sacred holy

siblings brothers and sisters

sickle a curved blade

symbol something that stands for or represents something else

Titanomachy in Greek mythology, the battle between the Titans and the Olympian gods

Titans a race of gods that ruled the universe before the rise of the Olympians

trident a three-pronged spear; it was one of the symbols of the sea-god Poseidon

versatile multitalented

SOURCE NOTES

Chapter 1
Greek Myth-Tellers Celebrate the Gods

Page 4, line 15: Hesiod. *Theogony*, in *Hesiod and Theognis*. Trans. Dorothea Wender. New York: Penguin, 1973, pp. 23–24.

Page 5, sidebar: Ibid., p. 26.

Page 8, line 6: Pindar. *The Odes*. Trans. C.M. Bowra. New York: Penguin, 1985, p. 206.

Page 11, line 6: Herodotus. *The Histories.* Trans. Aubrey de Sélincourt. New York: Penguin, 1981, p. 151.

Page 11, sidebar: Mark P.O. Morford and Robert J. Lenardon. *Classical Mythology*. New York: Oxford University Press, 2010, p. 3.

Chapter 2
The Rise and Fall of the Titans

Page 12, line 11: Ovid. *Metamorphoses*. Trans. Rolfe Humphries. Bloomington: Indiana University Press, 1967, p. 31.

Page 18, line 17: Hesiod. *Theogony*, p. 28.

Page 19, line 4: Ibid., p. 29.

Page 23, line 9: Quintus Smyrnaeus. *Fall of Troy*. Excerpted in Theoi Greek Mythology, "Titans." 8 April 2011. www.theoi.com/Titan/Titanes.html

Page 24, sidebar: Hesiod. *Theogony*, p. 45.

Chapter 3
Mighty Zeus and the Olympian Gods

Page 31, line 17: Ovid. *Metamorphoses*. Trans. Rolfe Humphries, pp. 93–94.

Page 35, line 10: Ovid. *Metamorphoses*. Excerpted in Rhoda A. Hendricks. *Classical Gods and Heroes: Myths as Told by the Ancient Authors*. New York: Morrow Quill, 1978, pp. 79–80.

Page 37, line 21: Hesiod. *Theogony*. Excerpted in *Classical Gods and Heroes: Myths as Told by the Ancient Authors,* pp. 38–39.

Chapter 4
A Vast Number of Minor Gods

Page 45, line 15: Michael Grant and John Hazel. *Who's Who in Classical Mythology*. London: Routledge, 2002, p. 292.

Page 52, line 11: Apuleius. *The Golden Ass*. Trans. P.G. Walsh. New York: Oxford University Press, 1995, p. 92.

Page 57, sidebar: *Orphic Hymn no.33 to Nike*. Excerpted in Theoi Greek Mythology, "Nike." 8 April 2011. www.theoi.com/Daimon/Nike.html

SELECT BIBLIOGRAPHY

Ancient Sources

Apuleius. *The Golden Ass*. Trans. P.G Walsh.
New York: Oxford University Press, 1995.

Hendricks, Rhoda A., ed. and trans., *Classical Gods and Heroes: Myths as Told by the Ancient Authors*.
New York: Morrow Quill, 1974.

Herodotus. *The Histories*. Trans. Aubrey de Sélincourt.
New York: Penguin, 1981.

Hesiod. *Theogony*, in *Hesiod and Theognis*. Trans. Dorothea Wender. New York: Penguin, 1973.

Knox, Bernard M.W., ed., *The Norton Book of Classical Literature*. New York: W.W. Norton, 1993.

Ovid. *Metamorphoses*. Trans. Rolfe Humphries.
Bloomington: Indiana University Press, 1967.

Pindar. *The Odes*. Trans. C. M. Bowra.
New York: Penguin, 1985.

Modern Sources

Allan, Tony, and Sara Maitland. *Titans and Olympians*.
New York: Time-Life, 1997.

Bellingham, David. *An Introduction to Greek Mythology*.
Secaucus, N.J.: Chartwell Books, 2002.

Fitton, J. Lesley. *The Discovery of the Greek Bronze Age*.
Cambridge, Mass.: Harvard University Press, 2001.

Grant, Michael. *A Guide to the Ancient World*.
New York: Barnes and Noble, 1986.

Grant, Michael. *Myths of the Greeks and Romans*.
New York: Plume, 1995.

Grant, Michael, and John Hazel. *Who's Who in Classical Mythology*. London: Routledge, 2002.

Hamilton, Edith. *Mythology*.
New York: Grand Central, 1999.

Morford, Mark P.O., and Robert J. Lenardon. *Classical Mythology*. New York: Oxford University Press, 2010.

Nardo, Don. *Greenhaven Encyclopedia of Greek and Roman Mythology*. San Diego: Greenhaven Press, 2002.

O'Sullivan, Maureen. *Greek Gods: An Iconoclast's Guide*.
Athens: Efstathiadis Group, 1985.

Stapleton, Michael. *The Illustrated Dictionary of Greek and Roman Mythology*. New York: Peter Bedrick, 1988.

INDEX

About the author

Noted historian Don Nardo specializes in the
ancient world and has published numerous
books about Greek, Roman, Mesopotamian,
and Egyptian mythology. He lives with his wife,
Christine, in Massachusetts.

The gods and goddesses of
    Greek mythology
Author: Nardo, Don.

Lexile Value: 1020L